THE LITTLE BOOK OF
WINE

Published in 2023 by OH!
An Imprint of Welbeck Non-Fiction Limited,
part of Welbeck Publishing Group.
Offices in: London – 20 Mortimer Street, London W1T 3JW
and Sydney – Level 17, 207 Kent St, Sydney NSW 2000 Australia
www.welbeckpublishing.com

Compilation text © Welbeck Non-Fiction Limited 2023
Design © Welbeck Non-Fiction Limited 2023

Disclaimer:

ISBN 978-1-80069-541-2

Compiled and written by: Charlotte Denne
Editorial: Victoria Denne
Project manager: Russell Porter
Design: Tony Seddon
Production: Jess Brisley

A CIP catalogue record for this book is available from the British Library

Printed in China

10 9 8 7 6 5 4 3 2 1

THE LITTLE BOOK OF
WINE

PRESSED TO PERFECTION

CONTENTS

Introduction

Red, white, sparkling or rosé – arguably no other alcoholic drink has had more impact on our society than wine. From its earliest iterations in Egyptian earthenware all the way to the eye-catching bottles we find lining supermarket shelves today, this heady drink has evolved from its use in religious rites along with culture, diet and society as a whole. And with millions of hectolitres produced and consumed worldwide, our love of fermented grape juice shows no signs of waning.

But wine is more than just a drink. Each bottle enlightens the senses and immerses the drinker in the places and stories that make each bottle unique. These are tales of terroir, of climate, soil and grape, woven together by the artistry and expertise of each winemaker and the love of their craft.

In this oenophile's guide we get to the heart of our love affair with wine. After taking a tour of its evolution through the centuries, we explore the art of vinification before tasting the fruits of all that labour – in moderation of course – and learn how best to drink (and appreciate) this most esteemed of beverages. As well as a whole caseload of quaffable facts and famous sayings about the nectar of the gods, there is also a glossary of useful wine terminology for the aspiring connoisseur, just in case you need a handy reminder during a particularly arduous tasting session.

So, sit back and pour yourself a glass as we heed the wise words of Ernest Hemingway, who famously said, "My only regret in life is that I didn't drink more wine."

CHAPTER
ONE

A Brief History of Wine

Tracing the cultivation of grapes for wine from Egypt to the present day

The drinking of wine
was first referenced in a
6,000-YEAR-OLD
document from ancient
Mesopotamia called the
"Hymn to Ninkasi".

Since then, this heady drink has played a significant role in many ancient civilizations, including Ancient Egypt, Greece and Rome.

The Egyptians considered wine a luxury and customarily offered it as a libation to the gods.

Typically stored in large clay jars called amphorae, these were often decorated with elaborate designs and hieroglyphics and sealed with mud or wax to prevent the wine from spoiling.

In Ancient Greece, wine
was seen as a gift from the
gods and was closely associated
with Dionysus, the god of wine
and fertility.

The Greeks believed that wine
had medicinal properties and
could be used to treat a variety
of ailments, such as fever and
digestive problems.

The Greeks had a tradition
of mixing wine with water,
which was seen as a mark of
civility and moderation.

The oldest known winery was discovered in a large cave complex in the village of Areni in the Vayots Dzor province of Armenia and is estimated to date back to around

4,100 BC.

During their excavations at the site in Areni, archaeologists found a fermentation vat carved into the rock floor, a wine press, storage jars, and a drinking cup.

In ancient Rome, wine was a staple of daily life and was consumed at all meals, including breakfast.

It was also used as a form of currency, with soldiers and government officials often receiving wine as part of their pay.

The Romans revolutionized the way wine was made and consumed when they developed the technique of aging wine in oak barrels.

Recognizing that the natural properties of the oak helped to improve flavour and texture, they began using oak barrels for wine storage and aging in around

200 BC.

The Romans first introduced grapevines to the UK in the 1st century AD, and established vineyards in what is now modern-day Kent, Essex and Sussex.

These vineyards produced wine that was exported back to Rome.

The importance of wine in religious and medicinal contexts during the Middle Ages led to a proliferation of vineyards and winemaking by monks and nuns throughout Europe, particularly in France, Italy, Spain and England.

Today, many of the world's most famous wine regions are still centred around monasteries and abbeys, reflecting the legacy of the Middle Ages.

The first recorded mention of sparkling wine was set down on papyrus in Ancient Egypt in 522 AD.

However, at that time fizzy wines were considered defective and unfit for trade so it wasn't until the medieval era that their development was first explored.

The Tudor era saw a significant expansion of wine production in England, with King Henry VIII establishing vineyards at Hampton Court Palace and other royal residences.

Red wine was the most popular type of wine in Tudor England, with claret (a type of red wine from Bordeaux) being a favourite among the aristocracy.

However, it wouldn't have tasted anything like the claret we drink today as wine was commonly fortified with alcohol and mixed with spices and herbs.

A Benedictine monk is credited as being the first to use a cork for sealing wine.

Previously stoppers had generally been made of wood wrapped in hemp soaked in olive oil.

The first European settlers to establish vineyards in the New World were the Spanish, who brought grapevines with them to Mexico and the southwestern United States in the 16th century.

In 1655 the Dutch colonial
governor of South Africa,
Jan van Riebeeck, planted
the first grapevines in the
Cape of Good Hope to
provide wine for sailors
on long voyages.

Portuguese port
was invented in the late
17th century when English
merchants began shipping
home Portuguese wine that
they fortified with brandy
to protect it from spoiling
while in transit.

The 17th century saw the emergence of the modern wine industry, with the advent of mass production and the use of glass bottles and corks.

In the late 1800s, French wines were almost lost forever when a tiny aphid-like insect called

PHYLLOXERA

spread across Europe causing widespread devastation to vineyards, particularly in France. Known as "The Great French Wine Blight", it led to the loss of countless grape varieties.

The solution to the crisis came from the discovery of a grafting technique, known as "grafting on phylloxera-resistant rootstocks", which saw European grapevines grafted onto certain American grape varieties that were resistant to phylloxera.

This process allowed for the recovery of many vineyards that had been decimated by the disease.

Australia and New Zealand both owe a debt of gratitude to James Busby, a British resident who arrived in

AUSTRALIA

in 1824 and established the first commercial vineyards in the Hunter Valley region of New South Wales.

Appointed to serve in New Zealand in 1833, Busby planted the country's first vineyard in the Bay of Islands.

After gold rush settlers
brought grapevines to

CALIFORNIA

during the late 19th and
early 20th centuries,
its wine industry grew
rapidly, and by the 1920s
it was producing more
wine than any other state
in the U.S.A.

The invention of stainless steel tanks in the 1920s revolutionized wine production by providing a clean and sterile environment for fermentation and storage.

Many French vineyards were heavily damaged or destroyed during World War One, which led to a shortage of wine.

In response, the French government established the "national wine office" (*Office national du vin*) in 1917 to regulate wine production and distribution.

During Prohibition some American wineries began producing "grape bricks" or "wine bricks" that could be sold legally as a food product.

These bricks contained concentrated grape juice that could be reconstituted into wine by adding water and yeast, enabling households to make their own wine at home.

In 1935 France developed the *Appellation d'Origine Contrôlée* (AOC) system to regulate the production of wine and protect the reputation of certain regions and vineyards.

There were basically two reasons France created the system of controlled appellations: phylloxera and fraud.

Michele Thomas, the assistant manager of Greene Grape Wine & Spirits in Brooklyn, New York.

In recent years, English sparkling wines have gained recognition for their high quality, often being compared to Champagne.

Many modern winemakers are using precision viticulture and computerized wine analysis to better understand their grapes and make more informed decisions about how to grow and produce their wines.

Some vineyards are also choosing to experiment with more sustainable farming practices and growing hybrids and ancient grape varieties that have fallen out of favour.

According to the latest available data from the International Organisation of Vine and Wine (OIV), the United States consumes the most wine of any country in the world, and Italy is the world's largest wine producer in terms of volume.

In 2020, Italy
produced an estimated

**47.5 MILLION
HECTOLITRES**

of wine,
followed by France with

**43.6 MILLION
HECTOLITRES**

and Spain with

**37.3 MILLION
HECTOLITRES.**

CHAPTER
TWO

Nectar of the Gods

From grape to glass, all you need to know about wine making

Wine is made from grapes, but not all grapes are suitable for winemaking.

There are over

10,000

grape varieties, but only a few hundred are used to make wine.

Vitis vinifera
(the common grape vine)
is the principal wine-
producing plant, and most
of the world's wine comes
from varieties of this
species, primarily because
of its high sugar content.

Grapes grown in warm, sunny climates ripen faster and accumulate higher sugar levels, giving wine full-bodied and fruity flavours.

Grapes grown in cooler climates have less opportunity to produce natural sugars and so tend to have higher acidity levels, which result in wines with a crisp and more refreshing taste.

Varietal characteristics and the geography of the growing region both play a significant role in the taste of a wine.

❦

Therefore, the choice of grapes grown by winemakers will depend largely on their location.

Many vineyards are located
on slopes because they provide
good drainage and can help
to protect the vines from frost
damage, as cold air tends to
settle in low-lying areas.

Slopes also offer good exposure
to sunlight which is essential
for the ripening process.

Winemaker Jean-Michel Comme of Château Pontet-Canet in Bordeaux implemented biodynamic practices throughout the vineyard after noticing that the areas where his cows preferred grazing produced better grapes.

A bottle of wine
contains approximately

600–800

grapes.

The timing of the grape harvest is key to ensure that the grapes are at their optimal ripeness, with the desired balance of acidity and sugar content.

High-quality winemakers tend to favour handpicking their harvest, as this allows the pickers to select only the ripest grapes and avoid damaging the fruit.

Once the grapes are sorted and any debris removed, they are crushed to release the juice.

❧

Some winemakers use an alternative method called whole-cluster fermentation, where the grapes are fermented with their stems.

After the grape juice
has been collected, it is
fermented using yeast.

Yeast inoculation is a critical
step in the winemaking
process as it converts the
sugar in grapes into alcohol,
giving wine its characteristic
flavour and aroma.

During its primary
fermentation the grape juice
and yeast mixture is placed in
fermentation vessels, which can be
made of stainless steel, concrete
or oak, and the vessels are kept at
temperatures of between

10 AND 27 DEGREES CELSIUS

depending on the type of wine
being produced.

Fermentation can last
anywhere from a few days to
a few weeks, and sometimes
includes a further process
of maceration (the practice
of leaving wine in contact
with skins, stalks and seeds),
depending on the grape variety
and intended flavour profile
of the wine.

Winemaker Randall Grahm of Bonny Doon Vineyard once tried to replicate ancient winemaking techniques by fermenting grapes in cowhides.

The resulting wine was reportedly quite funky.

In some cases, a secondary fermentation process called malolactic fermentation may be used to reduce acidity and soften the wine's flavours.

Aging wine also helps to enhance its complexity.

One of the most common ways to age wine is by storing it in oak barrels.

The type of oak used, such as French oak, American oak or Hungarian oak, and whether it is new or used, aids in the development of the wine's unique flavour and aroma.

Oak barrels also allow for slow oxygenation, which can help to soften the tannins in the wine and create a smoother mouthfeel.

Some winemakers choose
to age their wine in stainless
steel tanks which can help to
preserve fruit flavours and
acidity; others opt to age their
wine after bottling.

❧

Bottle aging can help a wine
to develop more complexity
and can be especially beneficial
for high-tannin red wines like
Cabernet Sauvignon.

It is essential to maintain consistent temperature and humidity levels during the aging process.

Temperature fluctuations can cause the aging wine to expand and contract, which can lead to oxidation and spoilage.

Before bottling, some winemakers choose to put their wine through a fining and filtering process to remove any sediment or impurities.

This can involve the use of substances like egg whites, bentonite clay or activated carbon.

Winemakers close their bottles depending on the style of wine and its aging potential.

A cork closure is best suited to a wine intended to age for several years as this enables controlled regulation of oxygen exchange.

In contrast, a wine suited to being consumed young is better suited for a screw cap closure that provides a tighter seal.

CHAPTER
THREE

Happy Hour

*Bold and fruity facts to keep
the wine conversation flowing*

The world's oldest bottle
of wine was discovered in a
Roman tomb in Germany in
1867 and is known as the
Speyer wine bottle.

Believed to date back to the
4th century AD, making it over
1,600 years old, the bottle
is sealed with wax and there is
still liquid inside.

Benedictine monk Dom Pérignon is often wrongly credited with inventing Champagne.

In 1662 Dr Christopher Merret, a member of the Royal Society, recorded the experiments of English cider and winemakers who were adding sugar to cider to create a bubbling drink.

This predates Dom Pérignon's literature on bubbling champagne.

Ever wondered why we "drink to one's health"?

Because in Ancient Greece, to show that the wine served to guests wasn't poisoned, the host would always take the first sip.

The tradition of clinking
glasses before drinking wine
dates back to ancient Rome,
where it was believed that
the sound of clinking glass
warded off evil spirits.

The oldest grape variety still in use today is thought to be the Assyrtiko grape, which is native to the Greek island of Santorini and has been used in winemaking for over **3,000 YEARS.**

More wine was exported in 2021 than in any year since records began, with shipments totalling

111.6 MILLION HECTOLITRES.

The population that consumes the most wine per capita is... Vatican City!

Residents reportedly drink

74 LITRES

of wine per person a year, which is double the per-capita consumption of Italy as a whole.

The most widely planted wine-making grape variety in the world is Cabernet Sauvignon, which is used to make many of the world's most expensive wines, including Bordeaux wines.

Wine bottle sizes from smallest to largest

Split: 187.5 ml, or a quarter of a standard 750 ml bottle

Half bottle: 375 ml, or half of a standard 750 ml bottle

Bottle: 750 ml, the standard size for most still wines

Magnum: 1.5 L, or the equivalent of two standard bottles

Double Magnum (Jeroboam in sparkling wines): 3 L, or the equivalent of four standard bottles

Jeroboam (Burgundy wines): 4.5 L, or the equivalent of six standard bottles

Rehoboam: 4.5 L, or the equivalent of six standard bottles (used mostly for Champagne and sparkling wines)

Methuselah (Imperial in Bordeaux wines): 6 L, or the equivalent of eight standard bottles

Salmanazar: 9 L, or the equivalent of twelve standard bottles

Balthazar: 12 L, or the equivalent of sixteen standard bottles

Nebuchadnezzar: 15 L, or the equivalent of twenty standard bottles

The largest sizes are the
Melchior (18 L), **Solomon** (20 L),
Sovereign (26.25 L) and **Primat**
(27 L), but these are relatively
rare and not commonly used by
modern winemakers.

The most notable wine
of the 20th century is
widely considered to be the
1976 vintage Chardonnay
from Napa Valley's
CHATEAU MONTELENA,
which won the "Judgment
of Paris" wine competition
in 1976, beating many
renowned French wines
from Burgundy.

The world's largest wine bottle was created by the Austrian winemaker Ghega in 2010. It held

490 LITRES

of wine and was over

2 METERS TALL.

Champagne Pol Roger created their Prestige Cuvée in homage to Sir Winston Churchill, mindful of the qualities that he sought in his Champagne: robustness, a full-bodied character and relative maturity.

The term

"OENOPHOBIA"

refers to a fear or hatred
of wine.

Red wine is often served at room temperature, and yet in fact most red wines should be served slightly below room temperature, at around

12–18 DEGREES

Celsius.

A "corked" wine doesn't mean there is a fault with the cork.

It means the wine has been contaminated with a chemical compound called TCA (2,4,6-Trichloroanisole), which can give the wine a musty, mouldy taste.

Wine tasting involves four senses: sight, smell, taste and touch.

The way a wine feels in your mouth (known as "mouthfeel") is an important part of the tasting experience.

In terms of wine, the "legs" refer to the streaks that form on the inside of a glass after you swirl it.

Contrary to popular belief, legs don't give any indication of quality.

If you spot the word
"vintage" on a wine label,
it refers to the year the
grapes were harvested,
not the year the wine was
bottled or released.

The first recorded
female winemaker was
Cleo, a Greek woman
who lived around

400 BC.

She was known for her
skills in winemaking and
was praised by Aristotle
for her ability to produce
excellent wines.

Champagne bottles are thicker and heavier than regular wine bottles to withstand the pressure of the carbonation.

Cleopatra, the last pharaoh of Ancient Egypt, was said to have enjoyed drinking wine infused with rose petals.

Edgar Allan Poe's
"The Cask of Amontillado"
features a character who
is walled up alive in a wine
cellar while drinking a cask
of Amontillado sherry.

Of the

10,000

registered grape varieties,
just 13 comprise a third of the
global vineyard surface, while
33 occupy 50% of the total.

Focus OIV 2017 Report on Global Vine Diversity

CHAPTER
FOUR

Wine O'Clock

How to train your nose and palate, with tasting notes on popular grape varieties

Let the wine breathe before drinking, even just for a few minutes, as this can help to soften the tannins and make the wine taste smoother and more balanced.

This is especially important for red wines. Lighter-bodied red wines, such as Pinot Noir or Beaujolais, may not need as much time to breathe as fuller-bodied red wines, such as Cabernet Sauvignon or Syrah.

Serve wine at the
right temperature.

As a rule, white wines
should be served chilled,
while red wines should be
served at slightly below
room temperature.

Serving wine at the wrong temperature can completely alter its intended taste and aroma. If a wine is served too cold its complexity may be muted, while if it's served too warm it can taste overly alcoholic or tannic.

Don't fill your glass
right to the top.

Pour wine to about a
third of the glass to allow
enough space for the
aromas to concentrate near
the top and hit your nose
when you first take a sip.

Swirl the wine in the glass
to aerate the wine and
release its aromas.

of taste comes from smell
and the different scents
released from the wine
will help you to experience
nuances that you might not
have otherwise noticed.

The shape and size of your wine glass can also affect your perception of how the wine tastes and smells.

A glass with a narrow opening, such as a flute or a tulip-shaped glass, can concentrate the aromas and direct them toward your nose, making it easier to smell the wine. In contrast, a wide bowl and a large surface area can expose more of the wine to the air, allowing it to breathe and develop more complex flavours.

Wine is a complex drink
with a variety of characteristics
that appeal to different people
in different ways.

When sommeliers drink
wine, they use all their senses
to evaluate the wine's quality,
character and potential.

However, the best way to
drink wine is in the way you
most enjoy it.

All wines should be tasted; some should only be sipped, but with others, drink the whole bottle.

Paulo Coelho

Wine can enhance the flavours of your favourite dishes, and vice versa.

Experiment with new food and wine pairings to extend your enjoyment.

Many winemakers use
a blend of several grape
varieties to create a unique
flavour profile, while some
prefer to use only one type
of grape to showcase its
unique characteristics.

Cabernet Sauvignon

Loved for its high concentration and age worthiness, Cabernet Sauvignon is the world's most popular red wine grape.

This full-bodied red wine boasts vanilla and dark fruit flavours and savoury tastes from black pepper to bell pepper.

"

An elegant and refined Cabernet Sauvignon with aromas of black fruits, graphite, and tobacco. The palate is full-bodied with silky tannins and flavours of blackcurrant, cassis, and dark chocolate. The finish is long and smooth.

"

Fiona Beckett, writer and food journalist, on Heitz Cellar Trailside Vineyard Cabernet Sauvignon 2014 (Napa Valley, California)

Chardonnay

Known as a winemaker's grape, the green-skinned grapes of the Chardonnay vine adapt to a variety of climates and are easy to work with in the cellar.

Its flavours range from apple and lemon to papaya and pineapple, and it also throws out hints of vanilla when it's aged with oak.

Elegant with understated oak and a subtle hint of creaminess on the nose. The palate is beautifully balanced with a silky texture and layers of ripe pear, apple and a delicate mineral note. The finish is long and refreshing.

Fiona Beckett, writer and food journalist, on Gusbourne Guinevere Chardonnay 2018 (Kent, England)

Pinot Noir

A versatile grape that can be made into a variety of wine styles, Pinot Noir is prized for its delicate aromas and flavours, which can include cherry, raspberry, strawberry, and earthy notes such as mushroom and truffle.

66

This is a classic Burgundy Pinot Noir, with aromas of cherry, raspberry, and earthy notes. The palate is medium-bodied, with flavours of red fruit, spice, and a hint of mineral. The tannins are firm but well-rounded, giving the wine a long, elegant finish.

99

James Suckling, wine and cigar critic, on Louis Jadot Gevrey-Chambertin 2018 (Burgundy, France)

Sauvignon Blanc

Known for its crisp and vibrant character, Sauvignon Blanc is often made into a varietal wine, meaning that it is produced using only Sauvignon Blanc grapes. Described as having flavours of citrus fruits, green apples, gooseberries, and grassy or herbaceous notes.

66

A masterful example of the classic Marlborough style. Zesty and fresh with intense aromatics of passion fruit, lime, and green apple. The palate is crisp and lively with a pure and focused finish.

99

Matthew Jukes, wine taster and writer, on Greywacke Sauvignon Blanc 2020 (Marlborough, New Zealand)

Merlot

A key component of many
Bordeaux blends, Merlot wines
are typically medium-bodied
with a soft, rounded texture
and can range from fruity
and easy-drinking to more
complex and structured with
hints of chocolate, vanilla, and
sometimes herbs or spices.

"

A stunning example of Pomerol Merlot with a complex and layered aroma of black fruits, tobacco, and cedar. The palate is rich and full-bodied with silky tannins and a long, spicy finish.

"

Matthew Jukes, wine taster and writer, on Château La Fleur de Gay 2016 (Pomerol, Bordeaux, France)

Bacchus

Often referred to as the UK's answer to Sauvignon Blanc, the Bacchus vine originated in Germany and is best suited to cooler climates. Bacchus wines can achieve both a fresh yet rich flavour. At typical sugar levels the grapes and resulting wine have elderflower aromas, but at higher sugar levels the flavours become more exotic.

"

A classic Bacchus, delivering intensely floral aromas with characteristically bold elderflower flavours along with crisp layers of citrus and apricot on the finish.

"

Clare Holton, Vineyard Manager at
Brissenden Vineyard, on Brissenden English
Bacchus 2018 (Kent, England)

Pinot Gris

Depending on the ripeness of the grapes, Pinot Gris produces wines that can range from light-bodied and crisp to full-bodied and rich often with flavours and aromas, of citrus fruits, apple, pear and sometimes tropical fruit.

66

This is a delightful example of Pinot Gris from New Zealand. On the palate, it is medium bodied with a lovely balance of fruit and acidity. There are flavours of pear and stone fruit, with a touch of spice and a long, fresh finish.

99

Jamie Goode, wine journalist, on Esk Valley Pinot Gris 2020 (Hawke's Bay, New Zealand)

CHAPTER
FIVE

Nunc est Bibendum

Memorable quotes from notable and unexpected oenophiles

"

In victory, you deserve Champagne.
In defeat, you need it.

"

Napoleon Bonaparte

Wine cheers the sad, revives the old, inspires the young, and makes weariness forget his toil.

Lord Byron

"

A bottle of wine contains more philosophy than all the books in the world.

"

Louis Pasteur

*My only regret in life
is that I didn't drink
more wine.*

Ernest Hemingway

"

Bordeaux is the wine of kings and the king of wines. It is a region steeped in history and tradition, and its wines are the benchmark for the world's greatest wines.

"

Matthieu Longuere MS, Master Sommelier and Wine Director at Le Cordon Bleu London

"

Age appears to be best in four things; old wood to burn, old wine to drink, old friends to trust, and old authors to read.

"

Francis Bacon

66

Wine is the most healthful and most hygienic of beverages.

99

Louis Pasteur

Wine is bottled poetry.

Robert Louis Stevenson

"

*Wine is a living
liquid containing no
preservatives. Its life cycle
comprises youth, maturity,
old age, and death.
When not treated with
reasonable respect it will
sicken and die.*

"

Julia Child

Wine is made in the vineyard and expressed in the winery.

Randall Grahm

"

*A bottle of wine begs
to be shared; I have
never met a miserly
wine lover.*

"

Clifton Fadiman

66

Champagne is the wine of celebration, the wine of kings, and the wine of eternal glamour.

99

Ronan Sayburn MS, Head of Wine at 67 Pall Mall

"

Wine is a constant proof that God loves us and loves to see us happy.

"

Benjamin Franklin

Wine is the only artwork you can drink.

Luis Fernando Olaverri

"

Drinking good wine with good food in good company is one of life's most civilized pleasures.

Michael Broadbent

66

Wine is sunlight,
held together by water.

99

Galileo Galilei

"

Wine is the most sensual and long-lasting of all the pleasures that nature has to offer.

"

Richard Best

*Wine is like people.
The great ones have
character, flaws,
and strengths.*

Bob Cabral

"

The winemaker's job is to celebrate the grape, not to orchestrate it.

"

Terry Theise

66

Wine is a reflection of its origin, its soil, its microclimate, its grape variety and its culture.

99

Leonardo LoCascio

"

*He who knows
how to taste does
not drink wine but
savours secrets.*

"

Salvador Dalí

Where there is no wine there is no love.

Euripides

Wine is one of the most civilized things in the world and one of the most natural things of the world that has been brought to the greatest perfection.

Ernest Hemingway

66

*Great wine begins in
the vineyard, and
it takes a dedicated
grower to coax
excellence from each
and every vine.*

Robert Parker

66

Wine is a very long and patient art. It does not like to be hurried or shocked.

99

Pierre-Auguste Renoir

Wine is the most beautiful and noble of all the arts.

Ernest Hemingway

CHAPTER
SIX

An Oenophile's Glossary

Words a wine connoisseur should know – and try to remember after a few glasses...

Aeration

The process of exposing wine to air, which can help to release its aromas and soften its tannins.

Aftertaste

The taste or flavours that linger in the mouth after the wine is tasted, spit or swallowed.

Appellation

A legally defined wine region
that has specific regulations
for grape-growing and
winemaking.

Biodynamic Wine

Wine made by following the biodynamic calendar and farming all components of the vineyard as one whole entity, eliminating the use of chemicals and using natural materials and composts.

Bite

A powerful initial sensation
of acidity or tannin when wine
is tasted.

Bouquet

The combined scents of a mature wine that have developed over time in the bottle.

Chef de Cave

French term for cellarmaster or head winemaker.

Claret

The British term for red wines
from Bordeaux.

Corked

A wine that has been
contaminated by a faulty cork,
characterized by a musty or
mouldy smell and taste.

Cru

A French term for a vineyard or wine estate that is known for producing high-quality wines.

Demi-Muid

A French term for 600-litre capacity oak barrels, typically used in the Rhône Valley.

Eiswein

Wine made from grapes that
have frozen on the vine.

En Primeur

Also known as Wine Futures, En Primeur refers to the process of buying wines before they are bottled and released onto the market.

Wines are purchased exclusive of Duty and VAT and then usually shipped 2-3 years after the vintage.

Enophile

A lover of all things vinous.

Fiasco

Traditionally used for the wines of Chianti in Tuscany, Italy, a fiasco is a rounded, bottom-heavy glass wine bottle partly covered with a straw basket at its base.

Finish

The lingering aftertaste of a wine.

Fortified

A wine that has had a distilled spirit, such as brandy, added to it to increase its alcohol content and stabilize it.

Gran Reserva

The highest level of Spain's quality categories, this distinction requires reds to be aged at least five years with a minimum of two in oak.

Grand Cru

French, literally "great growth",
describing the top tier of
vineyards and their wines in
regions that use the term.

Grand Vin

An unregulated term frequently used in Bordeaux to indicate that a wine is the best of multiple wines made at a given winery.

Hang time

The amount of time a grape
spends ripening on the vine.

Heady

Used to describe
high-alcohol wines.

Hectolitre

A quantity of liquid equivalent to 100 litres or 26.4 gallons.

In most of Europe, yield is measured in hectolitres per hectare whereas the U.S. use tons per acre.

Inoculation

The introduction of yeast to must during the winemaking process which kick-starts fermentation.

Kabinett

Literally means "cabinet", and is a German wine classification term that indicates that the wine is made from fully ripe grapes.

Kosher Wine

Wine made according to
Jewish dietary laws (the kashrut)
and certified by rabbinical
authorities.

Legs

The droplets or streaks of wine that form on the inside of a glass when it is swirled and liquid resettles to the bottom.

This phenomenon is determined by the wine's chemical composition and is affected by external factors such as temperature, humidity and the pouring vessel. It does not give an indication of quality.

Length

The amount of time that taste, flavour or mouthfeel persist after swallowing a wine.

The longer the finish, the better the wine quality. Common descriptors are short, long and lingering.

Magnum

A large bottle that holds the equivalent of two standard wine bottles.

Malolactic fermentation

A secondary fermentation process in which malic acid is converted into lactic acid, resulting in a softer, creamier mouthfeel.

Mouthfeel

The physical sensation of a wine in the mouth, including its texture, weight and astringency.

Must

The crushed grape juice and pulp
that is used to make wine.

Nose

The aroma or bouquet of a wine
that is detected by smelling it.

Oak

A flavouring agent that is often used in winemaking to add vanilla, spice and smoky notes to the wine.

Sommelier

A wine professional who is trained in all aspects of wine service as well as wine and food pairing.

Tannin

A natural preservative found in grape skins, stems and seeds that contributes to a wine's structure and bitterness.

Terroir

The environmental factors that affect a wine's character, including soil, climate and topography.

Varietal

A wine made from a specific type of grape.

Vintage

The year in which a wine's grapes were harvested.